A DK Publishing Book

Text Christopher Maynard
Project Editor Caroline Bingham
Art Editor Claire Penny
Deputy Managing Art Editor Jane Horne
Deputy Managing Editor Mary Ling
Production Ruth Cobb
Consultant Theresa Greenaway
Picture Researcher Tom Worsley

Additional photography by Max Gibbs, Steve Gorton, Frank Greenaway, Dave King, Susannah Price, Pete Gardner, Tim Ridley, David Rudkin, Clive Streeter, Philip Dowell

Published in Canada in 1997
by Scholastic Canada Ltd.,
123 Newkirk Road,
Richmond Hill, Ontario L4C 3G5

Copyright © 1997 Dorling Kindersley Limited, London

Canadian Cataloguing in Publication Data

Maynard, Christopher
Why are there waves?

(Why books)
ISBN: 0-590-24987-8

1. Water - Miscellanea - Juvenile literature.
l. Title. ll Series: Maynard, Christopher. Why books.

GB662.3.M39 1997 j553.7 C96-932331-X

Color reproduction by Chromagraphics, Singapore

Printed and bound in Italy by L.E.G.O.

The publisher would like to thank the following for their kind permission to reproduce their photographs:
t top, b bottom, l left, r right, c center, BC back cover, FC front cover
Bruce Coleman Collection: Nick de Vore (Why are there waves?)bl, (Why don't camels...?)c; **James Davis**: (Why does water freeze?)c; **The Image Bank**: G Brimacombe (Why does water turn to steam?)c; **Images Colour Library**: (Why do pebbles...?)cr, (Why do I sweat...?)tr, (Why can't I breathe underwater?)cl; **The National Trust**: Ian Shaw (Why is water like a mirror?)tr; **Pictor International**: (Why do pebbles...?)c; **Rex Features**: (Why do pebbles...?)bl; **Tony Stone Images**: (Why can't I breathe underwater?)c, BC cb, Lori Adamski Peek (Why do I sweat...?)c, Martin Barraud (Why are there waves?)br, John Lawrence (Why is water like a mirror?)c, Dennis O'Clair (Why can't I breathe underwater?)tr, James Randklev (Why does water turn to steam?)br, World Perspectives (Why are there waves?)cr; **Telegraph Colour Library**: FC cb, (Why are there waves?)c, endpapers

Questions

Why is water like a mirror?

Why does water turn to steam?

Why does water freeze?

Why do pebbles make ripples?

Why are there waves?

Why do I sweat when I run?

Why don't camels need
to drink everyday?

Why can't I breathe
underwater?

WHY
do volcanoes erupt?

Questions children
ask about the Earth

Scholastic Canada Ltd.

Why do stars

Seen from space, stars shine boldly. But starlight passes through a layer of air around the Earth before it reaches us. As this air moves, it makes the stars appear to twinkle.

Why is the Earth so blue?
From space the Earth appears as a big blue ball, smudged

twinkle?

white with clouds. This is because most of the planet is covered by blue water. Only one third is dry land.

Why do clouds float so high?

Clouds are made up of zillions of water droplets, each invisible to us and so light that they simply float in the air. Warmed by the sun, these rise high into the sky, like miniature hot-air balloons. Then they clump together to make clouds.

Why do people

We fall down, and not up, because of gravity. This force is created by the Earth, and it pulls everything very strongly down toward it. Without gravity, we would all float off into space.

Why can't we ski uphill?

It would be a funny sight if you whooshed uphill whenever you skied. You don't because gravity

fall downward?

Why do astronauts float?
Astronauts travel so high
and fast around the Earth
that they are able to
escape Earth's pull of
gravity. This means they
have no weight, so when
they step into space, they
float rather than
plummeting to the ground.

only pulls one way – toward the center
of the Earth. That's why you slide down
a mountain, not up to the top.

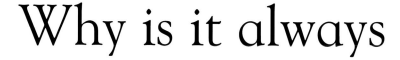

The North and South Poles lie farther from the sun than any other place on Earth. Because sunlight is weak there, they stay cold all year round.

Why are there jungles?
Jungles need two things to grow – lots of rain and lots of heat. At the equator, they get plenty of both. Here it rains almost every day, and in between the sun blazes down. This makes

icy at the Poles?

Why are there deserts?
Deserts are places that rain-bringing winds rarely reach. The rain may be blocked by mountains, so winds are often dry and suck up moisture. Really dry deserts may go as long as 20 years without rain.

an ideal environment for many plants and animals to make their home.

Why are pebbles

When waves crash onto beaches, they roll pebbles back and forth against

Why are cliffs dangerous?
A cliff face is exposed to the effects of ocean waves, wind, and rain. Under this constant attack, it can weaken and may collapse. That's why it's never a good idea to stand right on the edge of a cliff.

smooth?

each other. After years of rubbing, pebbles become worn, rounded, and smooth.

Why is sand so soft?

A grain of sand is actually as hard as a rock. But because the grains are so small, and the spaces between them full of air and water, they slide past each other smoothly and feel soft to walk on.

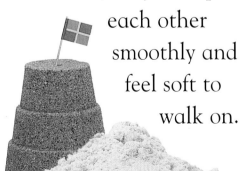

Why are there

Raindrops seep into the ground. If they find a soft rock called limestone, they eat away at it, forming little cracks

Why are there stalactites in caves?
Water drops leave tiny traces of a mineral called calcite on a cave's ceiling as they fall. Over thousands of years these accumulate, growing downward like icicles, to form hanging shapes called stalactites.

caves?

and holes. In time these grow bigger and bigger, and finally a cave is made.

Why do animals live underground?

Animals such as badgers and rabbits love to burrow down into soil. A burrow makes a cozy shelter and is a safe place to run and hide from a predator such as a fox.

Why do we find oil

Oil is made from plants that were buried in mud on the seabed millions of years ago. Eventually the mud changed to rock and the plants turned into the oil we now use for fuel.

Why do some rocks glitter?
Sometimes precious stones, called gems, are found in rocks. These are cut and polished to make them sparkle, then they are used for jewelry.

underground?

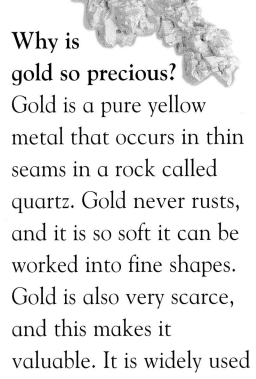

Why is gold so precious?
Gold is a pure yellow metal that occurs in thin seams in a rock called quartz. Gold never rusts, and it is so soft it can be worked into fine shapes. Gold is also very scarce, and this makes it valuable. It is widely used as a form of money.

Why do earthquakes

Earth's crust is made of giant plates that move against each other. If the plates get stuck, pressure builds up. It is released when the plates finally slip. The release is felt as an earthquake.

Why can't we dig through the Earth?
Deep underground there is so much pressure on the rock and soil that steel drills snap in two and holes close up as soon as they

happen?

are dug. At the very center of the Earth, it is so hot that rocks melt. There is no way through.

Why does the ground crack? If there is no rain for a long time, the ground begins to dry out as water turns into a vapor and is carried away in the air. This is known as evaporation. Cracks appear as the ground tightens and shrinks.

Why do volcanoes

Volcanoes exist at weak points in the Earth's crust. Active volcanoes act like giant plugs that hold back molten rock. Under this plug, pressure builds up until, eventually, the volcano explodes.

Why does lava flow?
Lava is rock that is so hot it melts. It blasts out of volcanoes when they erupt,

erupt?

Why are there mountains?

Mountains are like the rim of a pie crust. It only takes fingers to mold pie crust – Earth's crust is shaped by pressure on rocks deep within the planet. The pressure squeezes land together until it rises up to form mountains.

forming a burning orange river of fire. As soon as lava cools down, it hardens, forming dozens of different types of rocks.